S.P.O.R.T.S.

Smart People Only Read the Sports

By Jimmy "The Blueprint" Williams

S.P.O.R.T.S

Smart People Only Read the Sports

By Jimmy "The Blueprint" Williams

Cover by Donald Scott

Foreword by Devin McMillan

Copyright Page © 2015 by Moji

Publishing LLC

ISBN-13: 978-0692556528

ISBN-10: 0692556524

Published by

Moji House Publishing LLC.

PO Box 39776

Philadelphia P.A. 19106

Contents

7) You Soft Duke! (II)*

8) Kobe, OJ, Tiger and Mike Vick

9) College Age Restrictions

10) If You Dislike Boxing You Should Also Hate Prince's Music

11) Barry Bonds

12) P.I. = B.S.

13) Unwritten Rules are Tresvanty*

14) Wilt Chamberlain, Marilyn Monroe and The Table of
Gods

15) Bandwagon Fans

16) Mascots

17) Fantasy Football

18) Haters, Incest and Kendrick Lamar

www.WarRoomSports.com

<u>Acknowledgements</u>

Thanks to anyone who has ever listened to a podcast, watched a YouTube video, communicated with me on social media, or has met me anywhere offline. Even if you are one of the Jabronis who left an idiotic statement on the War Room Sports Facebook or Twitter pages, I thank you. To my family and friends; thank you for helping me become a genius shatner* talker. I have committed 10,000 hours to becoming a prolific shatner talker (Shout-Out To Malcolm Gladwell) and now I will put those thoughts in this book. I know people don't read these days but I'm still holding out hope that Jadakiss was wrong about you Neguses. And last but not least anyone who doesn't learn, laugh, or love any part of this book you should be aware you are a hater as well as a communist.

__Foreword__

Smart People Only Read The Sports. In our little bubble we call "the wild & wacky world of sports", we wholeheartedly believe this to be true. Sports is the world's greatest unite-r (I think I just made up a word), the most effective distraction from the trials and tribulations of everyday life, society's "common denominator", if you will. No matter what negativity plagues a person's personal life, society as a whole, or the world in general, that 2 to 4 hours you spend watching a game is an escape from the madness, and for that time, nothing else in the world matters. Admittedly, like the great LeBron James said (and I'm paraphrasing), after this contest is over, all of you will have to go back to your miserable lives. Though not the best thing to say by one of the most popular athletes on Planet Earth, LeBron couldn't have been more spot on. But what we do know, is unless your team is getting medieval-ly pasted during that few hour span, all the misery of the world ceases to exist while sports are on.

You know how you kids always talk about "keeping it real"? (That's ornery oldhead type talk right there. LOL) Well, at War Room Sports, without actually saying as much, that is our mantra in everything we broadcast. Opinions are spoken, no matter how popular or unpopular. We almost always miss the mark of political correctness. This book is no different. Birthed from the EXTREMELY "real" (and sometimes warped) mind of

Jimmy "The Blueprint" Williams, everything he says is definitely from the "IDGAF" section of his brain. But all-in-all, the way he looks at sports, culture, and life in general will keep you wanting more, and will definitely keep you laughing. If you don't hand this book to a friend, family member, or simply the person sitting closest to you at some point and ask them to read a passage you just finished reading, then I'll personally refund your purchase. (I will give you my address in Kabul, Afghanistan and you can swing by at any time to pick up your cash.)

The chapters you are about to read are not the things you'll find on your daily Sportscenter. It is simply the shit that was on "The Blueprint's" mind that he decided to put to paper for your enjoyment. I guarantee that some of these things have been on your mind at some point in life as well; you just never had anyone to discuss them with who'd give you a 100% honest opinion on them. Well now you do. While you're reading, just keep this one statement in mind…."Don't accept mediocrity and be steadfast in the war against ignorance". Enjoy S.P.O.R.T.S.

Devin McMillan

Preface

The first thing that should be understood is I am not a professional writer and I am not a professional sports journalist. Honestly I am just a sports, hip-hop, and television junkie that loves to talk shatner. Keep in mind while reading that I write the same way I talk and if you don't like it you can kiss my Ashton Kutcher* (No Skittles). You can take your judgment and apply it to your mother or your father (If you happen to know who he is). This book isn't meant to pontificate about religion or politics and I know some of you uppity jokers or Black Intellectuals or Religious Zealots or fake Hoteps that get your hands on my work will dismiss my thoughts but you're doing yourself and your country a disservice.

Sometimes I may discuss a serious issue followed by talking about the most ignant (yes ignant, not ignorant) topic you've ever heard discussed. That's because I'm honest. Yes I love to talk on an intellectual level but I also love ignance. Every morning I read The Wall Street Journal but I also check Worldstar and TMZ. I love Ashley & Jacquavis novels the same way I love reading Cornel West. So I don't have to answer whether it's Oochie Wally or is it One Mic, because it's both. No one is conscious or revolutionary 24/7 and if they are, stay far away from them because they are sick. I put this book together because it was on my bucket list to write a book and to get some people to read who usually don't read. I mean it's about sports and it's also intentionally not that long of a book. I mean "Who Moved My Cheese?" was only 96 pages, yet it was one of the most powerful books I've ever read. So there are no excuses not to read this, unless of course you can't read.

I listen to so much Hip-Hop that I find myself using Hip-Hop lyrics in conversation. As you read this masterpiece, you will realize that the way I see sports is not normal but it makes it more interesting. S.P.O.R.T.S. is by far the greatest sports book ever written. Well that is my opinion which you will notice is a common theme in this book. And also I named it "S.P.O.R.T.S." because I love acronyms (FOH* is the single greatest acronym ever). This book is a collection of essays that I wrote about various topics in sports. Many will disagree with my opinions and that's okay, as long as you have sound logic

behind your opinion.

I know it's an overused cliché but sports really is

a microcosm of life itself. I have been a huge sports fan

all my life but one thing I have noticed is that my

perception of sports and sporting events is not normal.

Most sports debates end up in arguments about stats,

championships, or athletic achievements. My arguments

end up in a discussion about Hip-Hop, Movies, Pop

Culture, or the feature page of Pr0nhub. This book is a

collection of my rants about different topics in sports,

which also reflect my unique way of appreciating sports.

I was tempted to write a fictional book but I instead

chose to write about my love (and hate) of certain aspects

of sports. Besides, if I wrote a story about a black guy

who grew up in the housing projects in San Francisco,

became a college football star at USC, one of the greatest

running backs in professional football history, marries a

white woman, becomes a movie star, gets accused of

murdering the white woman, beats the case despite tons of

evidence saying he was guilty, writes a book talking about

what he would have done if he did it, then gets arrested

for robbery trying to get back items stolen from him, goes

to prison, and while in prison decides to become a

television evangelist, you would think it was far-fetched

and completely impossible. You would probably say

"Jimmy, there's no way a Black man could get found not-

guilty of murdering a white woman when there is

evidence suggesting he did it". So with that in mind I decided to write about how smart people relate to sports. I am not saying if you don't watch sports you aren't smart, just that you can get a better understanding of the world and all of its complexities by watching sports. Sports has a unique way of dealing with complex issues such as race, religion, sexuality, economics, education, and in Shawn Kemp's and Travis Henry's case, birth control. I use a lot of War Room Sports colloquialisms so I have provided a War Room Sports Glossary at the end of the book to help you out. Keep in mind that these are my opinions and my opinions only, and if you dislike anything I have said just @ me. (@JWTheBlueprint)

Mike Schmidt & Jheri Curls

My obsession with sports started decades ago. While many of my friends growing up wanted to be Superman, Batman, or Spiderman; I grew up wanting to be Magic Johnson, John Elway, and Mike Schmidt. I later hated Mike Schmidt, in fact, it's possible that I still hate Mike Schmidt. Mike Schmidt is the reason I feel you should never meet your heroes. I met Mike Schmidt about 25 years ago and he was a total charlie*. Now he could have been having a bad day but I really didn't care then and I don't care now. You know what?; I just realized that I do still hate Mike Schmidt. I mean I don't hold grudges or anything but he was a total charlie that day. That day is why I hope I never meet Magic or Elway. Elway looks like he could be a total douche so it wouldn't shock me, but I think I'll keep my distance from Elway (No Skittles). If I met Magic and he acted like a charlie it would basically ruin my childhood. Magic was by far my childhood hero and I am an admitted Magic Johnson Stan. My War Room comrade PJ will tell you I got into fights on playgrounds defending Magic and there were many Jordan vs. Magic arguments that damn near came to blows. I'm not saying Jordan wasn't a better player than Magic but I do know Magic is a better human being who doesn't take advantage of kids in third world countries while enriching himself and doing nothing to help his own people. At any rate, I was never a comic book fiend like others because I was totally addicted to sports. I would take the paper as a little kid and read box-scores, and standings, and create crazy stories in my head about the games. When I was fairly young there was no Sportscenter (I know Sportscenter started in 1979 but I didn't have cable then. "I didn't grow up with a silver spoon in my mouth...Mizz Hawkins!"). In fact there wasn't even 24-hour TV. There was no Sunday Ticket or MLB Extra Innings, or NBA League Pass. This forced me to create how the games played out because I wasn't constantly bombarded with highlights of the games.

Damn I just realized I'm old AF...

Before my teenage years, baseball was my favorite sport, by far. I knew the batting average of every Phillie and was obsessed with the team. Too bad it had Steve Jeltz,

Von Hayes, Glen Wilson, and a bunch of other players you have never heard of. The team stunk but my grandfather had season tickets so we went to many games. This was a gift and a curse. I got to see how beautiful the game was. To this day I believe baseball is the best sport to watch live. Going to these games also allowed me to meet many professional players. I already talked about my experience with Mike Schmidt but that was nothing in comparison to the way Andre "The Hawk" Dawson treated me (Pause). Although I was a 10 year-old kid, he cussed me out when I asked for an autograph. Because of this incident I started to hate everything about the Chicago Cubs and people with Jheri Curls. I started to lose interest in baseball when I realized the players were all a bunch of charlies (I came to this conclusion based on meeting two players).

I fell in love with basketball at a very young age. I love basketball more than any other sport. At War Room Sports, basketball is damn near a religion. See I grew up in inner city Philadelphia and I didn't sling crack rock but I damn sure had a wicked jump shot. I became totally obsessed with basketball. I read books on the history of the sport, played day in and day out and intentionally went around trying to start basketball arguments. I would try to pick arguments about who is the greatest player with my older friends and family members as well as the old heads in the barber shop. The problem is growing up in Philadelphia it's not considered opinion but it's a fact that Wilt Chamberlain is the greatest to ever play the game. I will talk about Wilt later in the book but these arguments were important in how I view sports. See the old heads would tell me these crazy stories about Wilt and his athletic achievements in high school. There was no footage of these games so I had to listen to these stories and then use my imagination.

These childhood arguments as well as being obsessed and not having highlights constantly in my face forced me to use my imagination when thinking about various games in different sports. I don't see sports as pure athletic events. Each game tells a different narrative. There are good guys as well as bad guys (Schmidt & Dawson). There is drama, as well as comedy, and thrillers. There are sports fans who only care about numbers and there are sports fans who only care about wins and losses. Not that statistics and wins and losses aren't important but if that's all you care about you are missing out on what makes sports special.

Blame Joe Pisarcik

As stated on the War Room Sports website my favorite

teams are the Denver Broncos, Los Angeles Lakers, and

The Philadelphia Phillies. I'm not gonna pretend to like

hockey but if the Flyers ever win you will see me fronting

at the parade with all my Flyers gear on (meaning my one

Flyers hat). Many people often ask me how I became a

Broncos and a Lakers fan considering I grew up in

Philadelphia. No I am not a bandwagon fan and no I don't

switch teams on a daily basis. What many also find crazy

is I don't root against the Eagles or Sixers, even though I

am a Broncos and Lakers fan.

I have been a Broncos fan since 1984. This was a time

when only two games came on TV at a time on Sunday.

The local game (The Eagles) was on one station and the other was an AFC game. It wasn't the fact that the Eagles were a terrible team but they were extremely boring. Ron Jaworski broke his leg that season and he was replaced by someone named Joe Pisarcik. Not only did I consider the Eagles boring, I considered NFC football boring.

Meanwhile in the AFC there were young, exciting QB's throwing the ball almost every down. Dan Marino, John Elway, and Jim Kelly were changing the game. When it came to scheduling games, the Broncos, Dolphins, and Bills always seemed to be one of the teams in the AFC game of the week. All of my friends seemed to be Dan Marino fans. In fact, Dev of WRS to this day thinks Marino is the G.O.A.T. Dev and I have been arguing sports for years. We met in 1st grade and have always been sports junkies. That means I have known him for over 30 years. Damn I'm old AF. Since everyone was Richard Riding* Marino, I decided to be an Elway fan because he was more exciting with his ability to scramble and make plays. I also found it somewhat dope to root for a team no one I knew liked. When I told people I was a Broncos fan back then they looked at me crazy. The Broncos didn't win the Bowl that year. In fact they didn't go to the Bowl. They ended up losing to the Steelers. That season Marino seemed to break every passing record and the Dolphins went to the Bowl. They ended up losing to the 49ers, led by Joe Montana. Although I personally thought the NFC was boring, they had some historically great teams that seemed to win every Bowl. The NFC had the 49ers, Giants, Redskins, and Bears. I knew at the time they were great teams but they were still boring AF. They were like J Cole. I know J Cole is a dope emcee and he has lyrics but I find his albums boring AF. The NFC teams played tremendous defense and played "smash mouth" football. It was just so repetitive and boring. Just like J Cole shows he is a sensitive and humble cat and tells you how Jay-Z initially dissed him when he wanted a deal on every song. So there you have it, J Cole is the equivalent of 1980's NFC football.

It wasn't easy growing up a Broncos fan. The team ended up having success and making it to multiple Super Bowls, only to get embarrassed. Since I was one of the only

Broncos fans my friends knew, I got killed during those

Bowls. It got so bad I physically got sick after one Bowl

and missed a couple days of school (thanks Joe Montana).

To this day I have no idea how Elway got some of those

teams to the Bowl. This is why Elway is the G.O.A.T. in

terms of Quarterbacks (this isn't debatable). Since Al

Gore invented the internet, I have been able to meet

Broncos fans all across the world and even some in Philly.

The test of a true Broncos fan is to ask them how they felt

about 55-10. Their reaction will let you know if it's real.

I have also been a Lakers fan since the 80's. As I

mentioned earlier Magic Johnson was my childhood hero.

The way he played the game was just so amazing to

watch. I played organized basketball from the age of 8

and I always hated gunners. Magic had the ability to dominate games without scoring and he was one of the only players that truly looked like he was having fun. It was crazy being a Lakers fan in Philadelphia because they were somewhat rivals. The truth is the Celtics were more of a rival to both teams. That was also a reason I rooted for the Lakers. The Celtics and Lakers had a bitter rivalry which led to several Finals match ups. As a black supremacist, it was my job to root for the Lakers. I'm joking; I'm really not a black supremacist. I'm also not racist. I mean, I have several white friends. When I think about being a black supremacist it doesn't seem too bad though. I mean, what's wrong with thinking your race is superior. I guess the problem comes when you start to think you are superior in order to dominate and control another race, which is part of being a supremacist. And the word supremacist is always used in the pejorative anyway. When I think of a supremacist I think of men in white sheets and Bam Bam Bigelo. I'm not saying Bam Bam Bigelo was a white supremacist but let's keep it real, he looked like one. So did the Big Boss Man for that matter, and his character was a prison guard, and we know that the prison industrial complex is a tool used by white supremacists. Anyway, anyone who tells you race didn't play a factor in the Celtics/Lakers rivalry in the 80's is either a liar or they don't tell the truth. This led to me being a serious Lakers fan. Friends used to tell me my love of Magic was creepy, yet these were the same guys who would later worship Jordan while buying all of his

overrated sneakers (except for the Jordan 11's which were

dope AF). I'm not gonna front, I am a Magic Stan. If you

didn't grow up in that era you wouldn't understand, but

those that watched him play live will get it. I was so

much of a fan that when he announced he was retiring due

to H.I.V., I had to stare at the ceiling. I think someone

was cutting onions in the room when I watched the

announcement though. Then again in today's culture it's

cool to say you are sensitive. I blame this on light-

skinned rappers like Drake and J. Cole. I'm not from this

generation so I'm sticking to my story of someone cutting

onions when I watched the announcement. Many people

say it's easy to be a Lakers fan due to the success of the

team. That's one way to look at it but we also suffer from success (S/O to DJ Khaled). There are just as many Lakers haters as there are bandwagon fans. I don't consider myself a bandwagon fan because although I became a fan due to Magic, I was also there for Sedale Threat, Nick Van Excel, Elden Campbell, Cedric Ceballos, Magic's terrible stint as a coach with Vlade Divac as his leading scorer, and also when we got swept out the playoffs by the Utah Jazz. That was especially disappointing because my brother Kyree loves the Jazz and always has. He might be the only African American Utah Jazz fan not living in Utah.

The truth is, even though the team had success, I suffered

through a lot of terrible seasons as both a Denver Broncos

fan and a Lakers fan.

Dirk Nowitzki, Derrick Rose, Ronald Reagan

& Pro-Choice

I once read an article in *Philadelphia Magazine* by Janine White where she states "Each generation thinks the one preceding it is out of touch and the subsequent one self-entitled and lazy". I felt like this was an accurate statement and after one particular conversation I know it was an accurate statement. I argue sports on a daily basis and sometimes I get a good debate and other times I feel like I am wasting my time. What I've come to realize is, many of the younger generation of sports fans do not appreciate the history of the game of basketball. They act like basketball was invented by Jordan himself. I recently had two debates that reaffirmed my belief in pro-choice.

After Dirk Nowitzki had a tremendous game 2 in the 1st round of the 2011 NBA playoffs, a sports fan who shall remain nameless told me that Dirk was better than Larry Bird. I won't respond with résumés because the thought of Dirk being better than Bird is downright egregious! I'll just put it like this; Bird and Magic had the two highest basketball IQ's of all the players I have ever seen play! This same sports fan then proceeds to tell me that Derrick Rose is just as good as Jordan! Again I won't give you résumés; in fact I don't feel like I should say anything. At this point in our conversation I knew this guy was either a test-tube baby, a crack baby, or he just had the IQ of a bar of soap! The more I thought about it; I realized I don't blame young people for the way they think. It's our fault. We should have taught them better. We should have told them about the history, we should have taken them to the Gucci store to show them The Loafs. These young fans don't know any better and it's because they didn't have proper guidance. They didn't have anyone to teach them to respect the history of the game, or how to appreciate the small nuances in the sport, or why they should appreciate Darlene on the cover of Ice T's Power album. Instead they learned about sports while playing NBA live or 2K and Madden. This made me appreciate the sacrifices my family made for me in terms of education and making sure I had proper guidance. See, I attended an all-black private school so not only was I exposed to

teachers and faculty who gave me a sense of pride, which
these youngsters don't have, but I also don't suffer with
feeling inferior to others. These are the same kids who
grow up and practice respectability politics even though
#BlackLivesMatter, and you shouldn't have to pull your
pants up and wear a tie to avoid getting shot. I was taught
to appreciate all history and cultures. In fact, shout-out to
my 5th grade teacher Dr. Cooper, who encouraged me to
write and also told me "writing is a form of expression"
so it's okay to use slang and write on my terms. So in a
sense he's responsible for this amazing piece of work. So
although I get mad at times at sports fans from this
generation, it's really not their fault.

Respecting the history of the sport is important. I don't know what the NBA would be like if not for the players who paved the way for players like Dirk and Derrick Rose. I respect the elders and their contributions to the game and I believe they would be just as dominant if not more dominant today. Could you imagine what the NBA would be like without Magic, or without Bird or without Jordan? I mean, "What's Alex Haley if he doesn't have Roots?" Also, "what's a weekend if ya ain't knocking boots?" I don't want to know but the bottom line is respect the history of the game. I don't have a mercurial temperament but sometimes when talking to idiots I feel the need to use pejorative language. So for anyone out there who thinks it's okay to compare Derrick Rose to

Michael Jordan as of April 2015, do the world a favor and get neutered before you produce another ignorant creature that walks the earth spewing nonsense. Then again it's not their fault. It's actually Ronald Reagan's fault. His dealing of narcotics as well as the "War on Drugs" removed most of the guidance from these young buls*. So now instead of getting into heated debates where I disrespect these kids and question whether they grew up in houses with lead paint, I just say "Damn You Reagan" and try to show them better.

You Soft Duke!

The sports I grew up watching were a lot tougher and a lot more competitive. Now I have nothing against sportsmanship but what I have been seeing lately is utterly ridiculous. Anyone who thinks sports hasn't changed over the last two decades is someone who is as dumb as a cheddar bay biscuit and they also wear tube socks with a suit. In the NFL you are not allowed to hit anybody without giving the NFL a rebate, in the NBA you are not allowed to have any emotion without hurting your team by getting a technical foul. In the NHL they are trying to eliminate hard hits, which is hilarious considering nobody watches the NHL to see how great a grown ass man can skate. I watched LeBron James go back to Cleveland and make jokes with his former

teammates after an offseason where he basically called

them all garbage. He chose to leave a team that won over

60 games to play with his two friends and a bunch of

players that wouldn't make it on the bus if this was an

And 1 try out, only to go back to Cleveland and get a

blumpkin for doing so. It is ridiculous. I see players in

football and basketball knock each other down and then

rush to pick up the player they just knocked down. WHAT

PART OF THE GAME IS THAT?!?!?! In the words of

the great poet Christopher Wallace, "You Soft Duke!" I

sit back and think of the "Bad Boy" Pistons or the Pat

Riley Knicks or Heat teams and imagine them picking up

a player they just knocked down. YEAH RIGHT! I sit

back and wonder what Buddy Ryan would have said if Andre Waters or Wes Hopkins would have picked up a wide receiver they just knocked down. That would have been an offense comparable to Colonel Nathan Jessup ordering the code red on William Santiago. I know why Sports have become this way. It's not just one reason; it's an amalgamation of free agency, corporate sponsorships, and athletes becoming brands themselves. When Tom Brady said he hated the Jets, I got excited and thought "that's the way it's supposed to be". Stop being politically correct and telling people what they want to hear! Tell your opponent you hate them and then do your best to defeat them. I guarantee if sports stopped being so soft, the contests would mean more to the athletes and us as fans would get better contests. More players should be like Tom Brady and hate their opponents. Then again Tom Brady wears Uggs so he is also soft (II).

Kobe, OJ , Tiger and Mike Vick

As much as I love sports there has always been one thing

that bothers me. (At this point you should realize there is

a lot more than 1 thing that bothers me). What bothers me

are people who can't separate a person off the field, court,

golf course or wherever they display their talent, from

their athletic displays of greatness. I thought about this

due to several recent conversations I've had. The first was

in reference to Kobe Bean Bryant. I was talking to

someone about how Kobe was a great player not only

now, but an all-time great. They looked at me with an

incredulous smile and told me he wasn't even a great

player now so how could he be an all-time great. When I

asked them why they felt that way they started to tell me

how he was arrogant, how he snitched on Shaq, how he violated a young woman in Colorado, and a bunch of other sanctimonious garbage that I always hear. When talking about Kobe, people invariably give the same response to why he isn't great so I wasn't surprised. The next happened while watching the NFL network. They were ranking the top 100 players of all time. When it came to talking about OJ Simpson, the gentleman going over his highlights admitted that OJ's off the field issues affected where he was ranked. Now I don't know whether or not OJ committed those heinous acts but at the same time I know he was a beast at running back. The third incident was after Mike Vick went out on a Monday night and committed heinous acts of his own but it was on the Redskins defense. After his historic performance, when talking about the game with someone, they started to tell me about how he was a murderer, a criminal, a disgrace and a bunch of other nonsense I won't repeat. Yes he has made mistakes but he has paid his debt and has moved on, so people should do the same. There are countless other incidents such as the ones I have mentioned but these three incidents made me realize that people are basically stupid. That's right, I said it, PEOPLE ARE IDIOTS!!; and for the most part they have no life of their own so they sit around and hold others to a higher moral standard than they hold themselves. I know it's difficult to separate the person from their craft, and I am not asking people to be myopic when looking at an athlete, but don't be so stupid and judgmental that you diminish their achievements because of their mistakes away from their sport. As long as these mistakes don't affect their game like Eldrick "Tiger" Woods, then don't let it affect your opinion when judging them as athletes.

What's next? Will we start to look at the sartorial dichotomy of an athlete and say they are not great because of it? If that starts then there is a myriad of athletes that would go from great to trash truck juice*. If you judge a player's athletic ability based on what he does outside of his sport, then you are probably the type of person that still rolls their boogies although they are grown. My point is, appreciate the athletes for what they do in their sport and make sure you have a life of your own so you don't have to worry about what these Richard Heads do

off their respective courts.

College Age Restrictions

I'm old enough to remember a time when college basketball players played all four years and developed their talent at the collegiate level before becoming a pro. Now I realize many of them had to take pay cuts to go to the NBA but that's a story for another day. I watched the UNLV team that won a national championship with Larry Johnson & Stacey Augmon, the Duke Team with Grant Hill & Bobby Hurley, and countless other teams throughout the late 80's and 90's that had upperclassmen as their leaders. I also remember when the floodgates opened and high school players such as Garnett, Kobe, and Dwight Howard skipped college altogether and went straight to the pros. When this happened, it produced a lot of bad basketball. Some of the games in the late 90's were so bad I would rather watch a cricket match between homeless, dyslexic women that smell like ceiling fan dust before watching some of those games. Many basketball fans wanted a change and the basketball purist moaned and complained like a pedophile being interviewed by a special victims unit. The rules were changed and now players couldn't go straight to "The League" but had to wait at least one year after their high school class had graduated before entering the NBA draft. This started the "1 and done" phenomenon. Players then pretended to be "student-athletes" as they made a one year pit stop at college before turning pro. Others decided to play overseas for a year before entering the draft. In my opinion the one and done rule is worse than allowing

players to go straight to the NBA out of high school. The

one year in college does nothing as far as player

development, and I highly doubt if these players honestly

take their studies seriously. Now the college game is

ruined. I only watch during the tournament because the

regular season games are as entertaining as watching

illegal aliens that smell like used Chevy impala rotors,

hang drywall. I'm a college graduate and I take pride in

the fact that I put in work to get my degree. Yes I am a

snob and I resent the fact that some people make a

mockery of education by pretending that SOME of these

athletes really are students. Let's call it what it is, which

is a minor league. It's a great deal for the NCAA because

they don't have to pay these athletes. I'm not saying the NCAA should pay players because I honestly don't know how that will work. My answer is not to force someone who doesn't want an education to stay in school but to invest money in the NBA's D-League and allow the players to go there and develop their skills. This will allow the people that really want to go to college to go and the people who have no business in the classroom will also have a place to go. This will also make me happy because it will cut down on the bad basketball and also eliminate the press conferences where college athletes speak and sound as though their English professor is Fantasia Barrino. Of course this will never happen because the NCAA is making too much paper. So I'll get used to watching the inferior product because I'm a hoops

fan and as much as I clown the leagues, I keep watching.

If You Dislike Boxing You Should Also Hate Prince's Music

I remember watching Victor Ortiz upset Andre Berto for the WBC welterweight title and something occurred to me. I haven't been this entertained watching a boxing match in years. Then when I thought more about it, I realized there was only one fight I wanted to see and we all know what fight that was; the sports equivalent to the Detox album. Mayweather vs. Pacquiao, or as they called it, #MayPac. The problem is, now that Floyd and Pac-Man have fought, what's next? Ladies and Gentleman, boxing is dead! And the crazy part is it's not for a lack of great fights. It's because no one gives a shatner about the sport. Not that there aren't die-hard boxing fans but for the most part no one cares. MMA, in my opinion, is a better combat sport and will continue to become the dominant combat sport unless boxing changes its business model. First off, there are 376 different title belts in boxing. Maybe not 376 but you get the point. I have actually attempted to research this (by research this I mean used Google and asked people on Twitter) and here is what I found. Boxing has four governing bodies and 17 weight classes; and no concrete number of belts, so I'm sticking with my number of 376. I have asked many boxing fans to name the champions in each weight class to no avail. I bet if I would have given them 24 hours with Google, Wikipedia, or Don King himself, they wouldn't be able to give me the correct answer. I can admit I am an MMA junkie and for years I have been trying to convert many boxing enthusiast, but I may not have to. The "Sweet Science" is doing a great job of killing itself. Many have been unwilling to say that boxing is dead just because they grew up watching it and because it has been around for so long. MMA is looked at by many as a niche sport that will never become mainstream. That's okay because basketball was once looked at in the same light.

Basketball is my favorite sport by far and if I never gave it a chance because it wasn't around long enough or because I grew up watching baseball, that would have been an unpardonable act. Sports must evolve with the time and boxing has not done so. It is possible for both MMA & Boxing to coexist but boxing must find a way to make the fights the fans want to see. The UFC has built a brand around MMA, and there is no boxing brand that is as recognizable. I thought Golden Boy would be that brand, despite the owner allegedly engaging in cross-dressing. Hopefully, Premier Boxing Champions will help us see the fights we want to see.

The crazy part is, the purses in boxing are still far superior to MMA and there have been some amazing fights over the last couple years, which should help the sport. People tell me that they don't care because the fights aren't heavyweights, so they don't care to watch. So now we won't appreciate greatness because of the size of the competitors (II)? This is why boxing is dead. Not just because of the sport, but because people are morons.

Should we not appreciate Prince or his music because he is shorter than the average woman? Prince is an amazing musician (still not better than Mike) and has a body of work that is considered legendary. The same people who say they don't watch because of the lack of heavyweights are the same jabronis who shell out money to watch Floyd watch every time, even though he is not a heavyweight.

WTF? I wouldn't be surprised if I found out that most of these people love "Purple Rain", although they shouldn't.

Barry Bonds

Want to piss a baseball purist off? Just mention the name Barry Lamar Bonds. They hate him and so does Uncle Sam. Federal prosecutors spent taxpayer money to prove that Barry lied under oath and my question is; what was the point? I understand the danger in allowing individuals to lie under oath, but seriously, why spend all this time and money going after Bonds? At the end of the day he was found guilty of obstruction of justice and the Jury was deadlocked on the perjury charge. I hope they are happy. No matter how much they try to tarnish Bonds, it doesn't matter. He may never get in the Hall of Fame, but so what! The Hall of Fame is a joke anyway. The best players are not in the hall of fame. And if you try and put an asterisk next to his single season HR record of 73 or his career total of 762, it won't matter. It happened and we remember it, so FOH! I'm not condoning Bonds sticking anabolic horse steroids in his ass, and I do realize that the "steroid era" will be frowned upon in the history books. But seriously, is there a need for Congressional hearings and perjury trials? Barry Bonds never kissed the media's ass and he acted like a jerk as he was breaking records and leaving the stadium "driving something red, like that horse standing on its hind legs" (Nas Voice). People couldn't stand this. He never answered the media's questions the way they wanted him to. So now you spend money just to prove he obstructed justice by not answering questions the way you wanted him to. LMAO! You could have given me a

check and I would have told you that Bonds is evasive

when answering questions, you varmints. I wonder how

much this prosecution cost in total? "I hope those creeps

got receipts." Where were the prosecutors over the last

decade as bankers ran this country into the ground and

hurt the American people, forcing them to lose their jobs,

homes, and retirement money? No financial executive

has been convicted, although for over a decade they have

been riding around in their "Marine Blue 6 coupes",

pillaging from the poor and middle class without fear.

Instead, the people who are supposed to protect us are

going after Barry Bonds and Lil Kim. How about going

after Lil Kim's plastic surgeon for his egregious practice

of medicine! Congress took the time to question financial executives and talk greasy to them but where was the action? Where were the perjury trials or criminal prosecutions? Mark Twain once said "Action speaks louder than words but not nearly as often." Sounds like he was speaking about Congress. And if you are one of those people who believe this trial will help clean up the game, I feel sorry for you. You are naïve and you probably mop floors for a living. Hey, it's nothing wrong with that, because next you will be washing lettuce, then you will be on fries, then the grill, and pretty soon you will make assistant manager…"and that's when the big bucks start rolling in". I know the black protectionists* will be emailing me and sending me tweets because I am dissing a Government run by Obama, but so what. And don't tell me I can't speak on this because I don't understand perjury and the justice system. If Ashley Judd can speak on Hip-Hop, then I also can have my opinion on this ridiculous hypocrisy. So next time I hear the government going after a steroid user, I hope there are bankers also being prosecuted. If not, the Government should fall back like LeBron's hairline.

P.I. = B.S.

The average fan watches football and enjoys the action,

the hard hitting (II), and all of the excitement, and

believes that NFL football is the greatest sport. It has

become America's favorite sport. But from an

existentialist point of view I believe that Pro Football is a

great game but there are certain rules that sometimes ruin

an entire game. Rarely will you hear me say NCAA

college football has it right, considering how many things

I personally believe they do wrong. But watching football

over the past couple of weekends has made me realize

they have at least one thing right, and that is the penalty

for defensive pass interference. In the college game, the

offense gets 15 yards and an automatic first down on

defensive pass interference. When you juxtapose that rule with the pro game, you will see what I mean. In the NFL when a defensive player is called for pass interference the offensive team not only gets an automatic first down, but they get the ball at the spot where the interference took place. THAT'S A JOKE! There is a problem with how the NFL handles pass interference on so many levels. First off, wide receivers are so much bigger than cornerbacks these days (II). All the rules are in favor of the wideouts, due to changes in the game. Also these 40 and 50 yard pass interference penalties are causing teams to lose games. Most of the calls made by the officials are subjective anyway; I mean if they wanted to, they could call holding on almost every play. With that being said, games shouldn't be lost due to bogus Pass Interference calls. I saw my own Broncos once get a 49-yard Pass interference call that helped them win the game. A 49-yard penalty? Seriously? Well I guess it's only right that later that season my Broncos lost a game to the Jets due to a bogus pass interference call on fourth down. If I were a struggling offense, I would just throw the ball up and force the zebras to make a call. This current rule is deplorable. I understand the NFL's need for scoring but for the biggest play of a game to be a pass interference call is asinine. I just hope a playoff game or Super Bowl isn't decided on a pass interference call. If it does, just remember you heard me complaining. With all that being said it could be worse. They could be like NBA refs.

Unwritten Rules are Tresvanty

I just want to say a few words about baseball and its
"unwritten rules". This has pissed me off for years.
Detroit Tigers pitcher Justin Verlander was working on a
no-hitter when Erick Aybar bunted the ball in the eighth
inning and reached first base when Verlander fielded the
ball and threw it wide to first base. Later in the inning a
two out single was hit and the no-hitter was broken up.
After the game many players were pissed at Aybar for
laying down the bunt when there was still a chance of a
no-hitter. They said he had broken one of baseball's
"unwritten rules". First off, the term "unwritten rules" is
stupid! If it's a rule, it should be in writing? Baseball
players overall are a bunch of bivious creatures. They

63

hate when players don't give their all by hustling to first

base or running on a pop-fly, but they get upset when

someone is doing everything in their power to get on base

when someone takes a no-hitter late into the game. Aybar

was trying to get on base late in a close game but because

Verlander had a no-hitter going on, you get pissed. If you

ask me it was a smart play, yet people were treating Aybar

like he was the leader of Cobra Kai, telling his students to

hurt Daniel-San. Baseball has so many unwritten rules

that players often break them without knowing. Jason

Turbow has written an excellent book called "The

Baseball Codes", which discuss some of baseball's

unwritten rules. Some of the rules are downright

egregious. I won't name them all but I want to mention a few so you can see how stupid they are.

1) Don't swing at the first pitch after back-to-back Home Runs. Huh? Why not? So if it is a good pitch to hit, I shouldn't swing because the pitcher sucks rhinoceros pizzle? That's just stupid!

2) When you are hit by a pitch, you shouldn't rub the mark. Even an average pitcher throws like 80 mph (don't quote me on that, I saw that stat watching little league). What if it hurts like hell?

3) Don't help the opposition make a play by bracing them if they are falling into the dugout. So basically, if you see a guy about to break his neck trying to make a play you

should just let him break his neck? I wonder how that will look on replay.

There are many more stupid "unwritten rules", but you get my point. I think baseball players should act like adults and stop being so "Tresvanty". They should take all of these unwritten rules and toss them in a pit of unfortunate. I find it funny how players speak out when someone breaks an unwritten rule, but for the most part they remain silent when a player breaks written rules. Where is the backlash when players get caught drinking & driving, or spousal abuse, or drug possession? Yet when someone lays down a bunt in the 8th inning of a close game, players want to speak up. For the players who spoke out against Aybar, you should be forced to drink bleach and then be thrown off the roof of a

Baltimore row home, landing on dog feces with glass in

it. And for those who read this and also believe in these

unwritten rules, you can get the Bozak! Link for dude's

book ------> http://www.amazon.com/Baseball-Codes-

Beanballs-Bench-Clearing-Unwritten/dp/0375424695

Wilt Chamberlain, Marilyn Monroe and The Table of Gods

Many of you know that unfortunately I am a 76ers season ticket holder and I once watched them lose to the Thunder while scoring only 88 points. The next game was against the Warriors and I was also in the building. That Warriors game was no regular game because it was the 50th anniversary of Wilt Chamberlain scoring 100 points in an NBA game.

That's right, 50 years after Wilt scored 100, the Sixers as a team didn't crack 90. That just goes to show you how dominant Wilt was as an NBA player. Wilt's numbers are so crazy that in The War Room we believe that he may have never existed. But the craziest part is 100 points in a game was not Wilt's most impressive stat. Check out his scorecard with the opposite sex and it makes his 100 points in a game seem like nothing. For you Michael Jordan Richard Riders, peep this; Jordan had 50 or more 31 times in his career, but Wilt did it 45 times in 1 season. Wilt led the league in scoring, rebounding, and won MVP as a Rookie. Wilt has many more unbelievable stats but I'm not gonna sit here and continuously give Wilt a blumpkin. You get the point. Do I think he is the greatest basketball player? Well, yes and no. I personally don't believe there is a "greatest" at any sport or position (II) on the field/court. I believe there is a table of Gods for every sport. What I'm saying is there are too many variables when it comes to judging players in team sports or individual sports against each other to determine who was greater. Rule changes, opponents, technology, level of tutes* available, Nike's budget etc. Therefore I believe there is a table which the best of the best can sit at and be crowned a God of their sport. (For anyone calling me blasphemous, **Funds On H**old). Wilt has a seat at the hoops table. So does Jordan, Magic, Kareem, Bill Russell, and "Shep" from Above the Rim. Yo, Shep gave out work in corduroys. Give that man his seat at the table! This Table of Gods concept works in Hip-Hop, politics, criminals, chefs, tutes, movies, actors, books, and a gang of other shatner. For instance, Bill Clinton sits at the Table of Gods for politicians because he was able to obtain arguably the most powerful office in the world while getting Blacks to vote for him, as he helped incarcerate their kids. (All while getting topped off on the clock). Marilyn Monroe is at the table of Gods for tutes for allegedly showing love to men from the political, as well as criminal table of Gods, all while making young women (to this day) admire and look up to her. Herrolll*??? How TF did we allow that? The bottom line is, as time passes on we can still acknowledge the people at the table while allowing other people to become Gods. I'm not saying I believe in polytheism because I know some people will read this and accuse me of that. I swear to the book Gods that will happen. Word to Apollo!

Bandwagon Fans

Bandwagon fans are the scum of the earth. It's not that they just jump onto the team that is having the most success currently, but it's the fact that most will never admit they are a bandwagon fan. A great example of this is grown men claiming to be Miami Heat fans, when they know damn well they never rooted for the Heat in their lives. If you never tried to help Alonzo Mourning when he needed a kidney, then you can't be a Heat fan. These same fans are now Cleveland Cavaliers fans now that LeBron broke up with D. Wade.

Here is the secret about being a bandwagon fan though. If you admit to being a bandwagon fan, people will respect you more. It's not the fact that you can't stick with one team and stand by them your entire life. I mean players and teams themselves aren't loyal so why should we be that way as fans. As an Alpha male it is against the unwritten rules (LMAO) for me to ever switch teams, but I would be lying if I said I'm as loyal as some of these die-hard fans out there. I mean, I root for my favorite teams but you'll never see me in face-paint and I won't get into a fight over my favorite team. The reason people hate bandwagon fans is because they are liars for the most part, and we know in the Bible it says if you lie, you cheat, and if you cheat, you steal. I really don't know if it actually says that in the Bible, but I know people take you seriously when you reference the Bible. I personally would rather reference Harry Potter but I don't remember

it being discussed in that great book. Not that the Bible

isn't a great book. Maybe not as good as Harry Potter but

it's ard*.

Mascots

As an adult, when I go to sporting events, at times I get irritated by the mascots. They run around, act a fool, and sometimes get in the way of the actual event. I sometimes wonder if they are even necessary.

Back in November (2010), the old Sixers and Flyers arena, The Spectrum, was set to be demolished. On TV, as they were showing footage from events in the arena, they flashed pictures of the old Sixers mascot, "Big Shot". I hadn't seen Big Shot in years because he had been replaced by a steroid using, hyperactive bunny named "Hip-Hop".

At the moment I saw Big Shot, all sorts of memories popped into my head. I thought of going to Sixers games as a kid with my father, uncle, or grandfather, and watching Dr. J and Magic put on performances that make the current NBA look like a minor league. I thought of watching Charles Barkley playing his heart out and intimidating players that were bigger, stronger, and faster than he was. I thought of watching Michael Jordan play live and putting the fear of GOD in Hersey Hawkins, just by looking him in the eye.

What I realized when I saw Big Shot was that he represented the moment when I fell in love with hoops. It wasn't the mascot itself, but the nostalgia they bring. So maybe mascots do play a part in the sports world. Maybe there are kids right now at Sixers games who are watching

Hip-Hop and are falling in love with the game. I doubt it though. Later in life when they see Hip-Hop they may think of Evan Turner stinking the place up or Elton Brand being abused by every other team's big men (II), or Andre Iguodala being asked to do more than he should. Good thing he went to Golden State and was utilized like he always should have been.

On second thought, maybe I should be giving credit to Dr. J, Maurice Cheeks, Moses Malone, Charles Barkley, Magic Johnson, Michael Jordan, Kareem Abdul-Jabbar, Larry Bird, and many of the legends I had the privilege of watching play at the Spectrum.

I guess mascots can represent both the good and bad. Unless of course we are talking about the Phillie Phanatic, because he kicks a$$ no matter how good or bad the

Phillies are.

Fantasy Football

I hate fantasy football. Yup! You read that right, I hate fantasy football. Don't get me wrong, I have participated in fantasy football since 1997. I've won championships in multiple leagues and have made money and lost a hell of a lot as well. My problem is; people who love fantasy football swear they are geniuses, when to be honest, most of it is luck. Also, it makes me watch God-awful games on random nights of the week, knowing I have better things to do, like discuss white supremacy on Twitter or watch fight videos on Worldstar. I find myself rooting against my favorite team because I need certain players to score. I know that sounds crazy but look, they get paid whether they win or lose and they don't give AF about me, really. There are levels to my blasphemy, though. I will never draft a Raiders player and root for him. It's against my religion. I don't care if Bo Jackson from Tecmo Bowl was available. Yes, I hate the Raiders; only because I hate their fans. They have fans that brag about Super Bowl wins that happened 20-30 years ago. GTFOH! Then they all look like they are unemployed weirdos who play dress up on Sundays. Call me a snob, but you must admit that Raiders fans look ridiculous at games. But I digress. Fantasy football is here to stay because as Americans we love to gamble, and football is the greatest sport to gamble on. That's American football, btw. S/O to all of my foreign readers but I call your sport Soccer. But some of you fantasy geeks have got to chill with your overanalyzing of the game and your fantasy teams. I have seen people win leagues without any research and I have seen people who literally call up front offices for info and still come in last place. And also, there is no way anyone can convince me that it doesn't alter the games. I know athletes as well as coaches have fantasy teams. How could they not, even if it's subconsciously, make decisions to benefit their fantasy team? I know I would. I know Pete Rose would. I know Tim Donaghy would.

I know how popular fantasy sports are now but the next time you are watching the bum a$$ Raiders playing the Jaguars on a Thursday night and you're cheering for a running back who should be playing semi-pro, remember you are part of the problem.

__Haters, Incest and Kendrick Lamar__

I pride myself on being an independent thinker. I think

that's one thing that is missing in education these days.

Children are not taught to be independent thinkers. This is

why when discussing sports many people regurgitate

whatever they've heard on Sportscenter. The crazy part is

people will argue you down about statistics and results of

games like you can't just go to Google and figure out that

they are full of shatner. This happens all the time and

when I point out that someone is foolish and they can't

respond, they sometimes just respond by calling me a

"hater". Explain how I'm a hater because you are

obviously the product of incest and therefore lack the

mental capacity to do something as basic as going to

83

Google. Not you, the reader, unless of course you are actually a product of incest. I mean, you could have a bright future. Things worked out well for King Joffrey Baratheon, depending on how you look at it.

I'm not saying there aren't haters who exist because I know several of them. They can be great people, especially those that understand they are haters and have no problem admitting it. You just can't call someone a hater because you disagree with them. Someone has to earn the title of being a hater. You can't just go throwing that title around all willy nilly like we do with "classic" or "legend".

This is just what we do in 2015. I can promise you that the next album Kendrick Lamar drops after To Pimp a

Butterfly will be "classic" because he's a "legend". (LOL) Not that I don't like Kendrick Lamar (ll), but 2.5 minutes after his album drops, I see people all over the world (Twitter) say it's a classic. How is an album classic in less time than it takes me to heat up my favorite Lean Cuisine? Don't hit me with the "instant classic" rhetoric either because I just don't believe in that. There are albums that I've loved and thought were all time greats, and after a couple months I forget they exist. Classics have to stand the test of time. It's the same with legends. People can say whatever they want about Wilt but his name is always mentioned when speaking of the greats. Also, I personally think "To Pimp a Butterfly" is overrated (not that it's not great). I think I like Kendrick the emcee more than I do his music (ll). Sonically it gets

boring and those alien voices he uses annoy me. I love

what he stands for though, so I hope he wins. I mean, I'm

not a hater.

Computers Putin' Theory

One of my favorite athletes to ever play the beautiful

game Dr. Naismith created was one Allen Iverson aka A.I.

aka the Answer aka Bubbachuck aka Jewelz. I know he's

made several mistakes in his personal life and on the

court, but none of that matters. For me, there are certain

athletes that are beyond slander, although I know they are

flawed. I mean, we are all flawed except Serena

Williams. Those athletes would be Mike Tyson, AI, and

Serena. This applies in all forms of entertainment. The

same way I take up for A.I. is the same way I take up for

Cam aka Cam'ron aka Flea aka…nevermind. The point

is, I know Cam gets "computers putin'", but that doesn't

matter. Cam is also one of the most entertaining, ignant,

and comical people in Hip-Hop. The same could be said for R. Kelly. I mean, Chocolate Factory is a classic (No Kendrick). He is also flawed and enjoys the company of teenagers, but his music is undeniable. Out of all the names I've mentioned, Iverson stands out for several reasons.

Iverson has several flaws but you also can't deny his ability as a basketball player. He has also been the reason for discussion about race in this country several times. All you have to do is watch the 30 for 30 on A.I. or even that terrible documentary that came on Showtime about Iverson to see how the incident at the bowling alley affected his life and also how crazy race relations were during that time in Virginia. I know you're saying "how could you watch that documentary on Showtime, it was

awful?" I agree it was awful but it was about A.I., so it

doesn't matter. It's what I call my "computers putin'

theory". Some people just get to the point where it

doesn't matter what they do or say, you're

such a fan you support and try and justify their actions.

Tyson could bite his opponent's ear, threaten to rape a

reporter, or talk about how he only does interviews with

women he fornicates with, and somehow I justify it. See,

I know this all sounds crazy but I'm honest. It's like I

said about bandwagon fans or even haters, as long as

you're honest, people should just respect it.

I remember when Iverson and the Sixers played that great

Lakers team with Kobe & Shaq in the NBA Finals. That

was a difficult series for me to watch because although I'm a Lakers fan, remember the "Computers Putin' Theory" doesn't allow me to root against Iverson. Somehow I got what I wanted as A.I. dominated the series but the Lakers still won. What was interesting about that series was the energy in Philly during the series. A.I. and the Sixers brought people together in the city. Everyone was so nice to me during that run. Usually in the city, we barely speak to each other when walking down the street. This isn't the South. The same thing happened in '08 when the Phillies won the World Series. I mean, I even had "Beckies" flashing me their mammary glands during the championship parade (which is why I will go to a Flyers parade, although I don't watch hockey). This is

why I can't deal with A.I. slander. I mean, even if you
don't respect his game, respect what he has done for race
relations. LOL

Battle Rap is a Sport

As I previously mentioned, I am not a sports journalist. I am however a sports blogger and podcaster, with many contacts in sports journalism. On a daily basis I have conversations with journalist about many different stories in sports. When I told them I would be covering battle rap like it's a sport they all laughed. What was funny to me was how ESPN can cover Poker or even The Scripps National Spelling Bee as a sport, but people laughed at battle rap. Now when I say battle rap, I'm not talking about what B. Rabbit did on 8 Mile (although he bodied Papa Doc), but I'm talking about the current culture/sport of battle rap that can be found in The URL, King of the Dot, The World Battle League, Don't Flop, and many other leagues. If you are not familiar, just go to YouTube and look up one of those leagues.

I've always thought that golf wasn't a sport because the outfit you wore during a game could be worn later for supper. I tried to play golf once and I realized how grueling it can be and also how physical the game can be. So yes, I have respect for golfers and now consider it a sport, but Poker and Spelling? (FOH)

Battle rap is much more of a sport than poker and spelling (even when Math Hoffa isn't involved). You have preparation, competition, physical exertion, skill, and it's highly entertaining. Some will argue that Poker and Spelling have the same. As Fredro Starr said in that classic piece of American cinema known as Strapped, "It ain't the same sandwich". Getting tired from standing up

spelling words isn't the same as having to write your

rhymes, do research, and prepare for what your opponent

might say, as well as dealing with the crowd. If you eff

up in battle rap you can get booed off the stage. If you

mess up in The Scripps Spelling Bee, no one will boo you

off the stage (although that would be hilarious).

Poker is interesting because everyone watching thinks

they can do better than the person they are watching. So

many people play poker and everyone believes they are

great and can beat the pros, which in essence allows the

pros to make a living by having novices come to the

casino to hand over their money. Most people who watch

battle rap understand the skill it takes to compete at the

highest level and understand they can't do it. It takes strategy to compete in battle rap in 2015. You know your opponent beforehand and must train and prepare the same way you would a boxing match. I've talked to battle rappers who physically train to prepare to stand on stage for a significant amount of time and also to help with breath control when delivering their lines.

When you watch the Olympics you will see even more madness in regards to what's a sport and what isn't. And now in 2015 there is a new sport called "Drone Racing". That's right, people are racing their drones and calling it a sport. In between giving tech companies all of our personal information, and sharing our every move with social media companies, we are now using drones so regularly that we started a sport racing them. We have become our own Big Brother. I don't know if George Orwell had this in mind. Drone racing doesn't take the same level of skill or have the same level of competition that battle rap does, so if that can be called a sport so can battle rap. And don't get me started on NASCAR. That is considered a sport, and Tony Stewart may have killed someone literally on a track, but he still "Ain't got Barz Like That". See what I did there?

Overrated Doesn't Mean You're Not Good

The term "overrated" is clearly subjective. I find it funny when I call something overrated that people come at my neck and call me a hater. You know how I feel about the term "hater". I also don't usually take the time to explain why overrated isn't always used in the pejorative but "I'ma keep it G Real with you, Today I got time Cuz". If you say someone is the greatest or the number one in anything and I think they are number 2, then in my opinion you are overrating them. That, by itself isn't a negative comment. I've had this argument countless times when I say Jordan, Tupac, Ebony Ayes, or The Godfather are overrated. Not that all of them aren't great at what they do. Jordan is definitely a top five player of

97

all time, but because I don't drink the Kool-Aid, or shall I say Gatorade that Nike has sold us, doesn't make me crazy. Think about all the people who have played the game of basketball. Now for me to say he is top five all time is more of a compliment than a diss. Tupac was an amazing poet, actor, and mind, but I honestly dislike more of his songs than I like. The thing is, the songs I dig, I really dig. Tupac still isn't in my top five and might not be in my top ten. He is however in my top twenty. That might be more of an accomplishment than top five in hoops, considering how many people rap. The time it takes you to read this chapter, I will get about three mixtapes sent to me to laugh at. Ebony Ayes is an amazing actress with amazing talents and she definitely paved the way for many other female "actresses". I have seen publications such as Complex say she is the number one black actress in her field. Complex, you definitely need more people! The Godfather is a great movie, no doubt, but the recognition it receives is laughable, considering all of the subsequent films, which are clearly better. Movies like Shawshank Redemption, Goodfellas, Inception, Belly, Booty Talk 52, or Memento. I love the Godfather and again I'm saying it's an all-time great, but I'd watch any of the movies just mentioned before The Godfather any day. Now at this point, I know you're thinking that this is nothing more than my opinion. Guess what? You're right. But my opinion is all that matters right now and besides, I started off by saying "The term "overrated" is clearly subjective."

Occupy Wall Street & The NBA

Growing up as a fan of history, I was always amazed at the marches and protest that lead to our country being what it is today. People have fought for their rights in seemingly every decade and the power is always in the people. Many of these fights are not taught in history class because school really isn't meant to educate. School is meant to make the rich richer, while preparing the masses to be mindless members of society who are afraid to question authority. We never learn about people fighting for better work hours or women fighting for the right to vote, and in terms of the black experience, we are only taught about the March on Washington. In fact, when it comes to Black history, all we're ever taught in

101

school is Harriet Tubman, Dr. King, Rosa Parks, and maybe, just maybe, a paragraph about Malcolm X. This is why the whole "Occupy Wall Street" (OWS) movement and the protests starting all over the country have been so interesting to me.

One of the buzz words when talking about the OWS movement is "The One Percent". This phrase refers to the wealth inequality in our country and how the masses (the ninety nine percent) deal with mistakes made by the one percent, and also how a majority of wealth in this country is owned and controlled by that one percent. As I watched the idiot box during the protests, I couldn't help but think, "damn, this is no different than most major sports leagues". I mean, going into any NFL season I can tell you with 76.9% accuracy who will make the playoffs

(At least 70%). We know that most of the wealth in the

NBA is held by a few teams and we know only a few

have the chance to win. And now in the NBA you have

players finally recognizing their value and deciding to

play with who they want, where they want. These 50

million dollar petersons* are exercising their rights and

people are pissed. That's because they work for the "one

percent". (LOL). It's amazing to me how many people

feel sympathy for the owners in these contract situations

with players. That's because we've all been sold a lie that

says if you work harder than anyone you can achieve the

"American Dream", and you too can become an owner. I

don't mean to be a dream shatterer (word to Big Pun) but

the game is rigged and you can work as hard as you want but it takes more than hard work to become one of the one percent. If you really believe all it takes is hard work, you must also believe that Sherman's Special Field Orders, No. 15 are still gonna be executed. There is more of a chance the sorry NFL or NBA team you root for will become a champion because the one percenters who own the teams will find a way to stop their 50 million dollar petersons from exercising control, and will find a way to keep their leagues competitive and profitable. I told you the game is rigged.

War Room Glossary

- Not all of the words in the glossary are in this book, and not all of our jargon is in this book. It changes daily and some of it is "Only Built For Cuban Linx".

(II) - Pause. (Looks like the pause button on a TV remote). "The Point guard was big for us tonight (II)."

Ard - Philadelphia slang meaning alright. "That pretzel tasted amazing. It was ard."

Ashton Kutcher - Ass. "Kiss my Ashton Kutcher".

Becky - A white woman. "He made it to the pros and now only has relationships with Beckies".

Big International Tender Chicken Hawk or sometimes a Chicken Hawk - Clever way of calling someone a B.I.T.C.H. "You acting like a Big International Tender Chicken Hawk Right Now"

Black Protectionist or BP's- Someone who defends an African American regardless of whether they are wrong or not, just because they are an African American. "He told me it doesn't matter whether he robbed the bank. He was forced to do it, due to his economic status!" That's an example of a BP!

Bul - Philly slang used to describe a male. "Anybody seen the bul from South Philly?"

Charlie Batch or Charlie - A female dog, otherwise known as a b!tch. "You acting like a real charlie Right now" or "He shot that ball like a Charlie Batch".

FOH - F*ck outta here. "You think a Lincoln is better than a Cadillac? FOH!"

Funds on Hold - Another way to express FOH. "McGrady is better than Kobe? Funds on Hold!" (Contributed by James Onque aka "The educated brother from the bank")

Gis - Another way to ask the question "What the f*ck is…?". "Gis she talking about?"

Herrolll - A sound made when you are confused or don't understand what someone is saying or has said to you. "I think David Wingate was a great NBA player. Herolll!" (This was taken from the character "Dudda Man" from the great piece of American Cinema known as New Jack City).

Jevity - Another way to say longevity. "Kareem put up those numbers because of his jevity."

Marshall Faulk - Another way to express Mother F*cker or to express F*ck. "This Marshall Faulker is crazy!"… or…"I don't give a Marshall Faulk what I said ninja!"

Ninja - Another word for N*gga. "Ninja Please!"

Peterson - Another word for slave. "Your job has got you working like a Peterson!" (Inspired by Adrian Peterson comparing NFL players to "modern day slaves").

Richard Rider - One who expresses their admiration to another too aggressively. In other words, a "D!ck Rider!" "Stop Richard Riding LeBron you Chicken Hawk". Could also call someone a "Richard Head".

Thed - The hooped earring dude. A nickname for Michael Jordan. "Thed is running the Bobcats into the ground".

Tute - One who performs sexual services in exchange for money. Also known as a Prostitute. "He needs to stop picking up Tutes on Broad Street!"

Trash Truck Juice or TTJ - Something or someone that stinks to the point they smell of the liquid that oozes off of trash trucks. "His jumpshot is Trash Truck Juice!" or "His batting stance is TTJ".

Tresvanty - Sensitive. (Inspired by the classic hit "Sensitivity" created by R&B legend Ralph Tresvant).

William Shatner or just Shatner - Sh!t or Feces. "I don't give a William Shatner what you say!" or "She don't know William Shatner!"

About The Author

Jimmy is One of The Talented Tenth, but he likes Black Timbs and Black Hoodies. He was given the nickname "The Blueprint" from a business partner years ago. He continued to use the nickname because when you search online for James Williams or Jimmy Williams, millions of people come up... But when searching for James "The Blueprint" Williams or Jimmy "The Blueprint" Williams, guess who comes up?

Jimmy loves Hip-Hop, Sports, and Technology. He is also a Battle Rap Junkie...

He is the Co-Founder of War Room Sports, as well as War Room Sports TV.

Jimmy is also the Host of <u>Operation Battle Rap</u>. This is the first Battle Rap recap show broadcast using Google Hangouts. We cannot say we are 100% sure about it being the first but we like being the first and we don't know of anybody else who has done it, so we are claiming it. Jimmy <u>also buys and sells real-estate in Philadelphia</u>...

In the words of the great Biggie Smalls aka Notorious B.I.G. aka Frank White aka Big Poppa aka (You Get The Point), "Money I Make Into Stocks and Real Estate Bitch"....